Password Keeper

By
Mystic Art Glitters

Dates to remember

January

February

March

April

May

June

Dates to remember

July

August

September

October

November

December

NAME:

WEBSITE:

USERNAME:

PASSWORD:

NOTES:

NAME:

WEBSITE:

USERNAME:

PASSWORD:

NOTES:

NAME:

WEBSITE:

USERNAME:

PASSWORD:

NOTES:

NAME:

WEBSITE:

USERNAME:

PASSWORD:

NOTES:

NAME:

WEBSITE:

USERNAME:

PASSWORD:

NOTES:

NAME:

WEBSITE:

USERNAME:

PASSWORD:

NOTES:

NAME:

WEBSITE:

USERNAME:

PASSWORD:

NOTES:

NAME:

WEBSITE:

USERNAME:

PASSWORD:

NOTES:

NAME:

WEBSITE:

USERNAME:

PASSWORD:

NOTES:

NAME:

WEBSITE:

USERNAME:

PASSWORD:

NOTES:

NAME:

WEBSITE:

USERNAME:

PASSWORD:

NOTES:

NAME:

WEBSITE:

USERNAME:

PASSWORD:

NOTES:

NAME:

WEBSITE:

USERNAME:

PASSWORD:

NOTES:

NAME:

WEBSITE:

USERNAME:

PASSWORD:

NOTES:

NAME:

WEBSITE:

USERNAME:

PASSWORD:

NOTES:

NAME:

WEBSITE:

USERNAME:

PASSWORD:

NOTES:

NAME:

WEBSITE:

USERNAME:

PASSWORD:

NOTES:

NAME:

WEBSITE:

USERNAME:

PASSWORD:

NOTES:

NAME:

WEBSITE:

USERNAME:

PASSWORD:

NOTES:

NAME:

WEBSITE:

USERNAME:

PASSWORD:

NOTES:

NAME:

WEBSITE:

USERNAME:

PASSWORD:

NOTES:

NAME:

WEBSITE:

USERNAME:

PASSWORD:

NOTES:

NAME:

WEBSITE:

USERNAME:

PASSWORD:

NOTES:

NAME:

WEBSITE:

USERNAME:

PASSWORD:

NOTES:

NAME: ____________________

WEBSITE: ____________________

USERNAME: ____________________

PASSWORD: ____________________

NOTES: ____________________

NAME: ____________________

WEBSITE: ____________________

USERNAME: ____________________

PASSWORD: ____________________

NOTES: ____________________

C
D

NAME:

WEBSITE:

USERNAME:

PASSWORD:

NOTES:

NAME:

WEBSITE:

USERNAME:

PASSWORD:

NOTES:

NAME:

WEBSITE:

USERNAME:

PASSWORD:

NOTES:

NAME:

WEBSITE:

USERNAME:

PASSWORD:

NOTES:

NAME:

WEBSITE:

USERNAME:

PASSWORD:

NOTES:

NAME:

WEBSITE:

USERNAME:

PASSWORD:

NOTES:

NAME:

WEBSITE:

USERNAME:

PASSWORD:

NOTES:

NAME:

WEBSITE:

USERNAME:

PASSWORD:

NOTES:

NAME:

WEBSITE:

USERNAME:

PASSWORD:

NOTES:

NAME:

WEBSITE:

USERNAME:

PASSWORD:

NOTES:

NAME:

WEBSITE:

USERNAME:

PASSWORD:

NOTES:

NAME:

WEBSITE:

USERNAME:

PASSWORD:

NOTES:

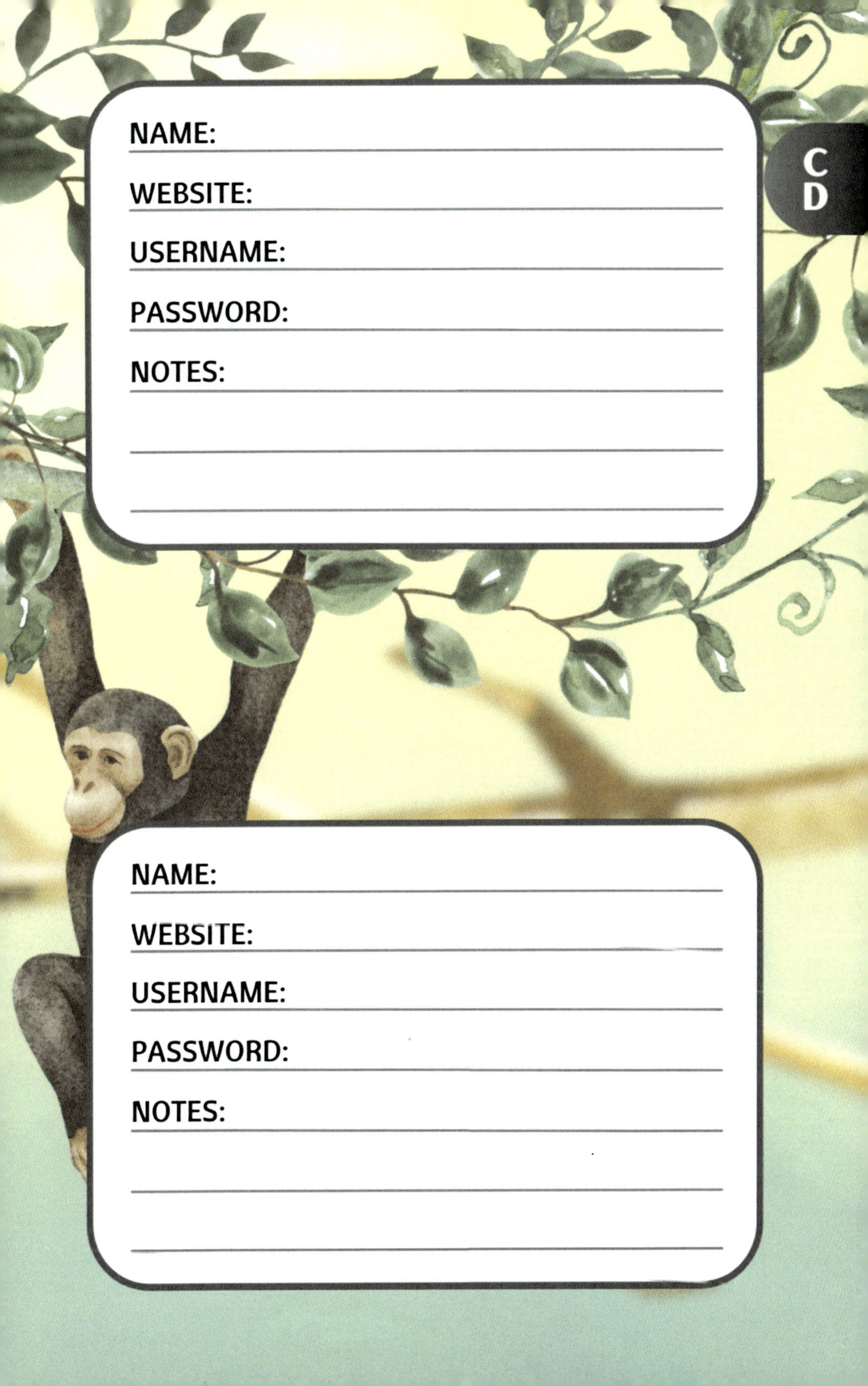

C
D

NAME:

WEBSITE:

USERNAME:

PASSWORD:

NOTES:

NAME:

WEBSITE:

USERNAME:

PASSWORD:

NOTES:

NAME:

WEBSITE:

USERNAME:

PASSWORD:

NOTES:

NAME:

WEBSITE:

USERNAME:

PASSWORD:

NOTES:

NAME:

WEBSITE:

USERNAME:

PASSWORD:

NOTES:

NAME:

WEBSITE:

USERNAME:

PASSWORD:

NOTES:

NAME:

WEBSITE:

USERNAME:

PASSWORD:

NOTES:

NAME:

WEBSITE:

USERNAME:

PASSWORD:

NOTES:

E
F

NAME:

WEBSITE:

USERNAME:

PASSWORD:

NOTES:

NAME:

WEBSITE:

USERNAME:

PASSWORD:

NOTES:

NAME:

WEBSITE:

USERNAME:

PASSWORD:

NOTES:

NAME:

WEBSITE:

USERNAME:

PASSWORD:

NOTES:

E
F

NAME:

WEBSITE:

USERNAME:

PASSWORD:

NOTES:

NAME:

WEBSITE:

USERNAME:

PASSWORD:

NOTES:

NAME:

WEBSITE:

USERNAME:

PASSWORD:

NOTES:

NAME:

WEBSITE:

USERNAME:

PASSWORD:

NOTES:

E F

NAME:

WEBSITE:

USERNAME:

PASSWORD:

NOTES:

NAME:

WEBSITE:

USERNAME:

PASSWORD:

NOTES:

NAME:

WEBSITE:

USERNAME:

PASSWORD:

NOTES:

NAME:

WEBSITE:

USERNAME:

PASSWORD:

NOTES:

NAME:

WEBSITE:

USERNAME:

PASSWORD:

NOTES:

NAME:

WEBSITE:

USERNAME:

PASSWORD:

NOTES:

NAME:

WEBSITE:

USERNAME:

PASSWORD:

NOTES:

NAME:

WEBSITE:

USERNAME:

PASSWORD:

NOTES:

NAME: ____________________

WEBSITE: ____________________

USERNAME: ____________________

PASSWORD: ____________________

NOTES: ____________________

NAME: ____________________

WEBSITE: ____________________

USERNAME: ____________________

PASSWORD: ____________________

NOTES: ____________________

NAME: ______________________

WEBSITE: ______________________

USERNAME: ______________________

PASSWORD: ______________________

NOTES: ______________________

____

____

NAME: ______________________

WEBSITE: ______________________

USERNAME: ______________________

PASSWORD: ______________________

NOTES: ______________________

____

____

NAME:

WEBSITE:

USERNAME:

PASSWORD:

NOTES:

NAME:

WEBSITE:

USERNAME:

PASSWORD:

NOTES:

NAME:

WEBSITE:

USERNAME:

PASSWORD:

NOTES:

NAME:

WEBSITE:

USERNAME:

PASSWORD:

NOTES:

NAME:

WEBSITE:

USERNAME:

PASSWORD:

NOTES:

NAME:

WEBSITE:

USERNAME:

PASSWORD:

NOTES:

NAME:

WEBSITE:

USERNAME:

PASSWORD:

NOTES:

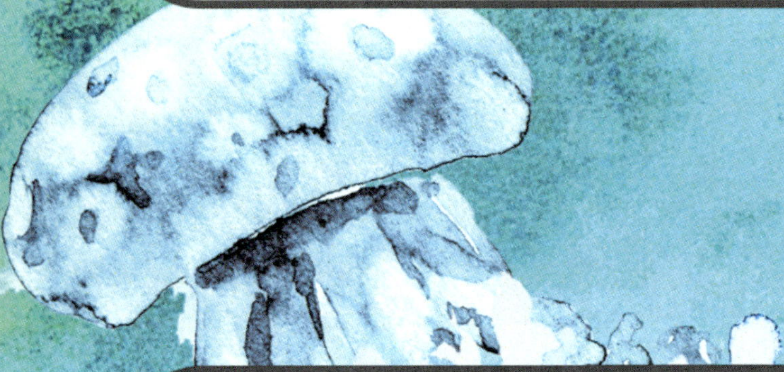

NAME:

WEBSITE:

USERNAME:

PASSWORD:

NOTES:

NAME:

WEBSITE:

USERNAME:

PASSWORD:

NOTES:

NAME:

WEBSITE:

USERNAME:

PASSWORD:

NOTES:

NAME:

WEBSITE:

USERNAME:

PASSWORD:

NOTES:

NAME:

WEBSITE:

USERNAME:

PASSWORD:

NOTES:

NAME:

WEBSITE:

USERNAME:

PASSWORD:

NOTES:

NAME:

WEBSITE:

USERNAME:

PASSWORD:

NOTES:

NAME:

WEBSITE:

USERNAME:

PASSWORD:

NOTES:

NAME:

WEBSITE:

USERNAME:

PASSWORD:

NOTES:

NAME:

WEBSITE:

USERNAME:

PASSWORD:

NOTES:

NAME:

WEBSITE:

USERNAME:

PASSWORD:

NOTES:

NAME:

WEBSITE:

USERNAME:

PASSWORD:

NOTES:

NAME:

WEBSITE:

USERNAME:

PASSWORD:

NOTES:

NAME:

WEBSITE:

USERNAME:

PASSWORD:

NOTES:

J

NAME:

WEBSITE:

USERNAME:

PASSWORD:

NOTES:

NAME:

WEBSITE:

USERNAME:

PASSWORD:

NOTES:

NAME:

WEBSITE:

USERNAME:

PASSWORD:

NOTES:

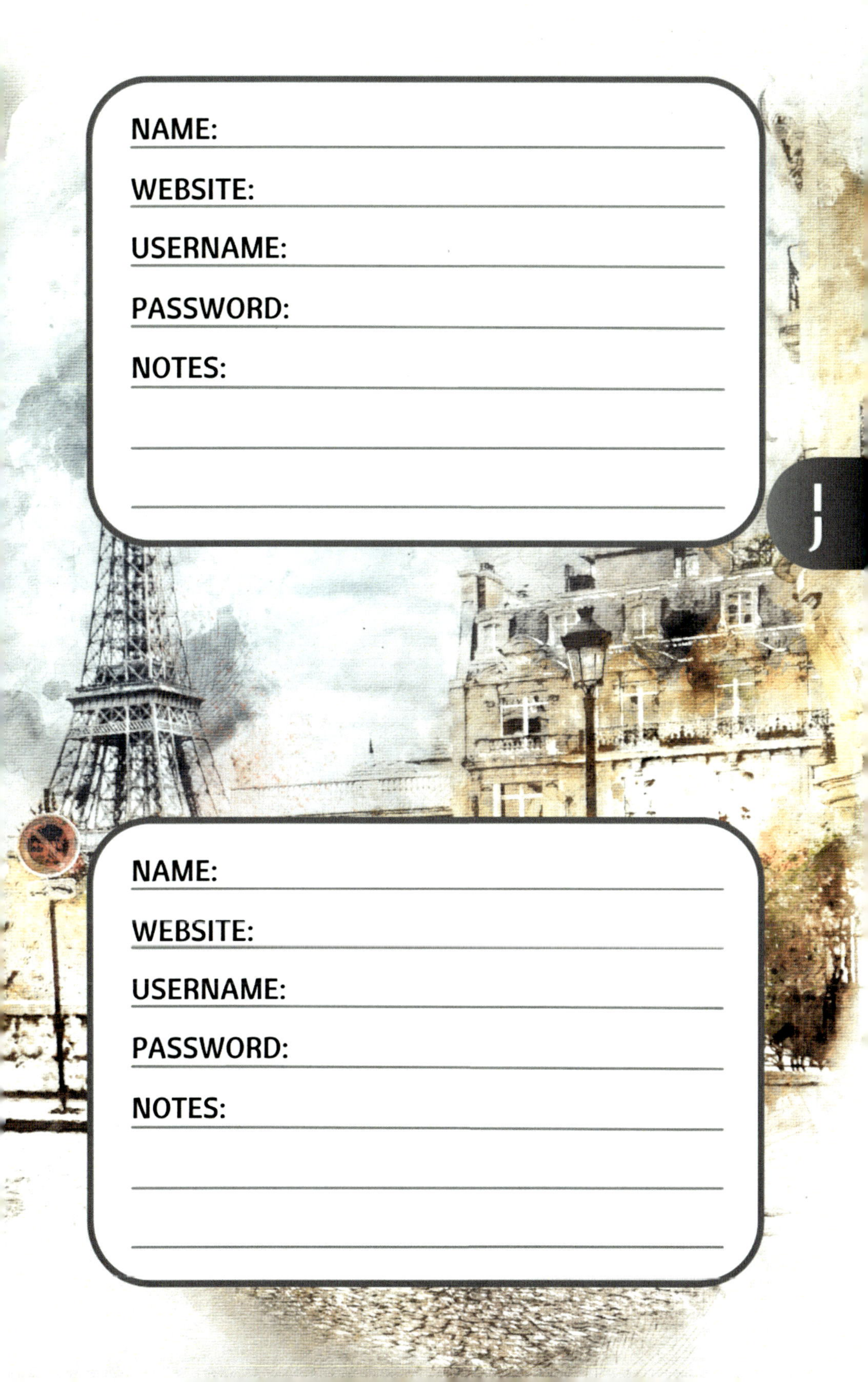

NAME:

WEBSITE:

USERNAME:

PASSWORD:

NOTES:

J

NAME:

WEBSITE:

USERNAME:

PASSWORD:

NOTES:

NAME:

WEBSITE:

USERNAME:

PASSWORD:

NOTES:

NAME:

WEBSITE:

USERNAME:

PASSWORD:

NOTES:

NAME:

WEBSITE:

USERNAME:

PASSWORD:

NOTES:

J

NAME:

WEBSITE:

USERNAME:

PASSWORD:

NOTES:

NAME:

WEBSITE:

USERNAME:

PASSWORD:

NOTES:

NAME:

WEBSITE:

USERNAME:

PASSWORD:

NOTES:

NAME:

WEBSITE:

USERNAME:

PASSWORD:

NOTES:

NAME:

WEBSITE:

USERNAME:

PASSWORD:

NOTES:

NAME:

WEBSITE:

USERNAME:

PASSWORD:

NOTES:

NAME:

WEBSITE:

USERNAME:

PASSWORD:

NOTES:

NAME:

WEBSITE:

USERNAME:

PASSWORD:

NOTES:

NAME:

WEBSITE:

USERNAME:

PASSWORD:

NOTES:

NAME:

WEBSITE:

USERNAME:

PASSWORD:

NOTES:

NAME:

WEBSITE:

USERNAME:

PASSWORD:

NOTES:

NAME:

WEBSITE:

USERNAME:

PASSWORD:

NOTES:

NAME:

WEBSITE:

USERNAME:

PASSWORD:

NOTES:

NAME:

WEBSITE:

USERNAME:

PASSWORD:

NOTES:

NAME:

WEBSITE:

USERNAME:

PASSWORD:

NOTES:

NAME:

WEBSITE:

USERNAME:

PASSWORD:

NOTES:

NAME:

WEBSITE:

USERNAME:

PASSWORD:

NOTES:

NAME: ______________________________

WEBSITE: ______________________________

USERNAME: ______________________________

PASSWORD: ______________________________

NOTES: ______________________________

____

____

NAME: ______________________________

WEBSITE: ______________________________

USERNAME: ______________________________

PASSWORD: ______________________________

NOTES: ______________________________

____

____

NAME:

WEBSITE:

USERNAME:

PASSWORD:

NOTES:

NAME:

WEBSITE:

USERNAME:

PASSWORD:

NOTES:

NAME:

WEBSITE:

USERNAME:

PASSWORD:

NOTES:

NAME:

WEBSITE:

USERNAME:

PASSWORD:

NOTES:

NAME:

WEBSITE:

USERNAME:

PASSWORD:

NOTES:

K
L

NAME:

WEBSITE:

USERNAME:

PASSWORD:

NOTES:

NAME:

WEBSITE:

USERNAME:

PASSWORD:

NOTES:

NAME:

WEBSITE:

USERNAME:

PASSWORD:

NOTES:

NAME:

WEBSITE:

USERNAME:

PASSWORD:

NOTES:

M N

NAME:

WEBSITE:

USERNAME:

PASSWORD:

NOTES:

NAME:

WEBSITE:

USERNAME:

PASSWORD:

NOTES:

NAME:

WEBSITE:

USERNAME:

PASSWORD:

NOTES:

NAME:

WEBSITE:

USERNAME:

PASSWORD:

NOTES:

NAME:

WEBSITE:

USERNAME:

PASSWORD:

NOTES:

NAME:

WEBSITE:

USERNAME:

PASSWORD:

NOTES:

NAME:

WEBSITE:

USERNAME:

PASSWORD:

NOTES:

NAME:

WEBSITE:

USERNAME:

PASSWORD:

NOTES:

NAME:

WEBSITE:

USERNAME:

PASSWORD:

NOTES:

NAME:

WEBSITE:

USERNAME:

PASSWORD:

NOTES:

NAME:

WEBSITE:

USERNAME:

PASSWORD:

NOTES:

NAME:

WEBSITE:

USERNAME:

PASSWORD:

NOTES:

NAME:

WEBSITE:

USERNAME:

PASSWORD:

NOTES:

NAME:

WEBSITE:

USERNAME:

PASSWORD:

NOTES:

NAME:

WEBSITE:

USERNAME:

PASSWORD:

NOTES:

NAME:

WEBSITE:

USERNAME:

PASSWORD:

NOTES:

NAME:

WEBSITE:

USERNAME:

PASSWORD:

NOTES:

NAME:

WEBSITE:

USERNAME:

PASSWORD:

NOTES:

NAME:

WEBSITE:

USERNAME:

PASSWORD:

NOTES:

NAME:

WEBSITE:

USERNAME:

PASSWORD:

NOTES:

NAME:

WEBSITE:

USERNAME:

PASSWORD:

NOTES:

NAME:

WEBSITE:

USERNAME:

PASSWORD:

NOTES:

NAME:

WEBSITE:

USERNAME:

PASSWORD:

NOTES:

NAME:

WEBSITE:

USERNAME:

PASSWORD:

NOTES:

NAME:

WEBSITE:

USERNAME:

PASSWORD:

NOTES:

NAME:

WEBSITE:

USERNAME:

PASSWORD:

NOTES:

NAME:

WEBSITE:

USERNAME:

PASSWORD:

NOTES:

NAME:

WEBSITE:

USERNAME:

PASSWORD:

NOTES:

NAME:

WEBSITE:

USERNAME:

PASSWORD:

NOTES:

NAME: ____________________

WEBSITE: ____________________

USERNAME: ____________________

PASSWORD: ____________________

NOTES: ____________________

____

____

NAME: ____________________

WEBSITE: ____________________

USERNAME: ____________________

PASSWORD: ____________________

NOTES: ____________________

____

____

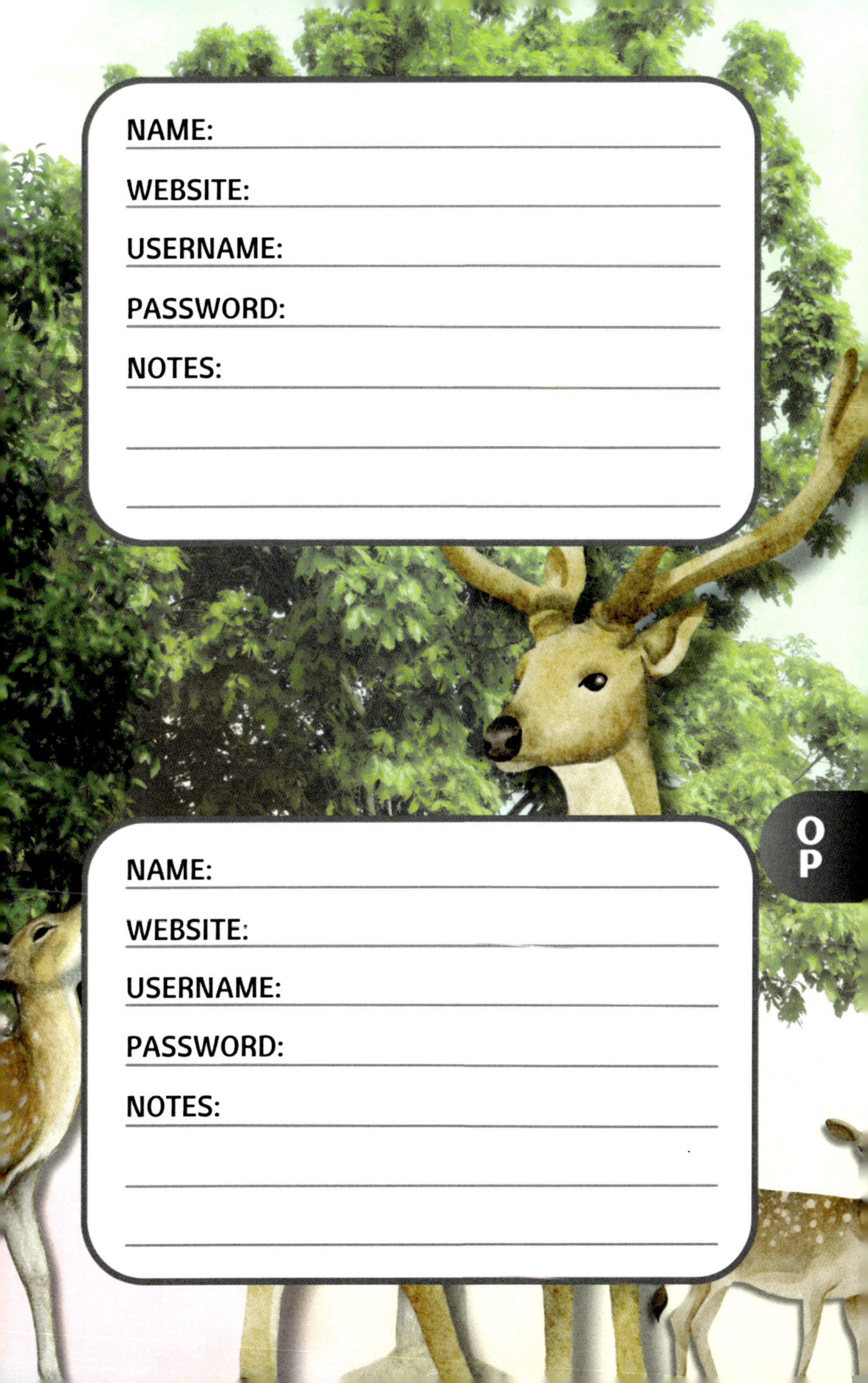

NAME: ______________________

WEBSITE: ______________________

USERNAME: ______________________

PASSWORD: ______________________

NOTES: ______________________

____

____

NAME: ______________________

WEBSITE: ______________________

USERNAME: ______________________

PASSWORD: ______________________

NOTES: ______________________

____

____

NAME:

WEBSITE:

USERNAME:

PASSWORD:

NOTES:

NAME:

WEBSITE:

USERNAME:

PASSWORD:

NOTES:

NAME:

WEBSITE:

USERNAME:

PASSWORD:

NOTES:

NAME:

WEBSITE:

USERNAME:

PASSWORD:

NOTES:

NAME:

WEBSITE:

USERNAME:

PASSWORD:

NOTES:

NAME:

WEBSITE:

USERNAME:

PASSWORD:

NOTES:

NAME:

WEBSITE:

USERNAME:

PASSWORD:

NOTES:

NAME:

WEBSITE:

USERNAME:

PASSWORD:

NOTES:

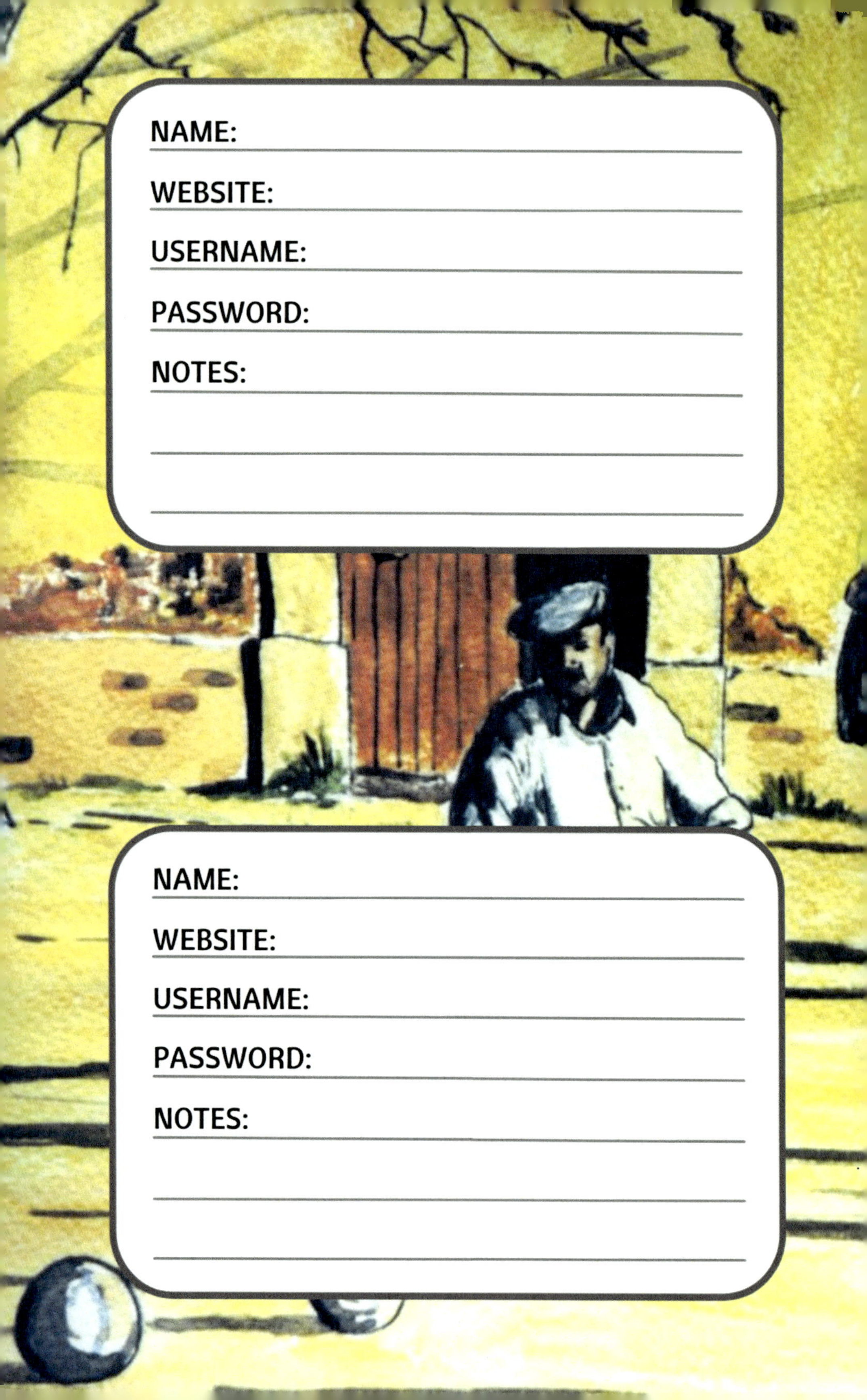

NAME:

WEBSITE:

USERNAME:

PASSWORD:

NOTES:

NAME:

WEBSITE:

USERNAME:

PASSWORD:

NOTES:

NAME:

WEBSITE:

USERNAME:

PASSWORD:

NOTES:

NAME:

WEBSITE:

USERNAME:

PASSWORD:

NOTES:

NAME:

WEBSITE:

USERNAME:

PASSWORD:

NOTES:

NAME:

WEBSITE:

USERNAME:

PASSWORD:

NOTES:

NAME:

WEBSITE:

USERNAME:

PASSWORD:

NOTES:

NAME:

WEBSITE:

USERNAME:

PASSWORD:

NOTES:

QR

NAME:

WEBSITE:

USERNAME:

PASSWORD:

NOTES:

NAME:

WEBSITE:

USERNAME:

PASSWORD:

NOTES:

NAME:

WEBSITE:

USERNAME:

PASSWORD:

NOTES:

NAME:

WEBSITE:

USERNAME:

PASSWORD:

NOTES:

NAME:

WEBSITE:

USERNAME:

PASSWORD:

NOTES:

NAME:

WEBSITE:

USERNAME:

PASSWORD:

NOTES:

NAME:

WEBSITE:

USERNAME:

PASSWORD:

NOTES:

NAME:

WEBSITE:

USERNAME:

PASSWORD:

NOTES:

NAME:

WEBSITE:

USERNAME:

PASSWORD:

NOTES:

NAME:

WEBSITE:

USERNAME:

PASSWORD:

NOTES:

NAME:

WEBSITE:

USERNAME:

PASSWORD:

NOTES:

NAME:

WEBSITE:

USERNAME:

PASSWORD:

NOTES:

NAME:

WEBSITE:

USERNAME:

PASSWORD:

NOTES:

NAME:

WEBSITE:

USERNAME:

PASSWORD:

NOTES:

NAME:

WEBSITE:

USERNAME:

PASSWORD:

NOTES:

NAME:

WEBSITE:

USERNAME:

PASSWORD:

NOTES:

S T

NAME:

WEBSITE:

USERNAME:

PASSWORD:

NOTES:

NAME:

WEBSITE:

USERNAME:

PASSWORD:

NOTES:

NAME:

WEBSITE:

USERNAME:

PASSWORD:

NOTES:

NAME:

WEBSITE:

USERNAME:

PASSWORD:

NOTES:

ST

NAME:

WEBSITE:

USERNAME:

PASSWORD:

NOTES:

NAME:

WEBSITE:

USERNAME:

PASSWORD:

NOTES:

NAME:

WEBSITE:

USERNAME:

PASSWORD:

NOTES:

NAME:

WEBSITE:

USERNAME:

PASSWORD:

NOTES:

NAME:

WEBSITE:

USERNAME:

PASSWORD:

NOTES:

NAME:

WEBSITE:

USERNAME:

PASSWORD:

NOTES:

NAME:

WEBSITE:

USERNAME:

PASSWORD:

NOTES:

NAME:

WEBSITE:

USERNAME:

PASSWORD:

NOTES:

NAME:

WEBSITE:

USERNAME:

PASSWORD:

NOTES:

NAME:

WEBSITE:

USERNAME:

PASSWORD:

NOTES:

NAME:

WEBSITE:

USERNAME:

PASSWORD:

NOTES:

NAME:

WEBSITE:

USERNAME:

PASSWORD:

NOTES:

NAME:

WEBSITE:

USERNAME:

PASSWORD:

NOTES:

NAME:

WEBSITE:

USERNAME:

PASSWORD:

NOTES:

NAME:

WEBSITE:

USERNAME:

PASSWORD:

NOTES:

NAME:

WEBSITE:

USERNAME:

PASSWORD:

NOTES:

NAME: ______________________

WEBSITE: ______________________

USERNAME: ______________________

PASSWORD: ______________________

NOTES: ______________________

____

____

NAME: ______________________

WEBSITE: ______________________

USERNAME: ______________________

PASSWORD: ______________________

NOTES: ______________________

____

____

NAME:

WEBSITE:

USERNAME:

PASSWORD:

NOTES:

NAME:

WEBSITE:

USERNAME:

PASSWORD:

NOTES:

NAME:

WEBSITE:

USERNAME:

PASSWORD:

NOTES:

NAME:

WEBSITE:

USERNAME:

PASSWORD:

NOTES:

NAME:

WEBSITE:

USERNAME:

PASSWORD:

NOTES:

NAME:

WEBSITE:

USERNAME:

PASSWORD:

NOTES:

NAME:

WEBSITE:

USERNAME:

PASSWORD:

NOTES:

NAME:

WEBSITE:

USERNAME:

PASSWORD:

NOTES:

NAME:

WEBSITE:

USERNAME:

PASSWORD:

NOTES:

NAME:

WEBSITE:

USERNAME:

PASSWORD:

NOTES:

NAME:

WEBSITE:

USERNAME:

PASSWORD:

NOTES:

NAME:

WEBSITE:

USERNAME:

PASSWORD:

NOTES:

NAME:

WEBSITE:

USERNAME:

PASSWORD:

NOTES:

NAME:

WEBSITE:

USERNAME:

PASSWORD:

NOTES:

Made in the USA
Las Vegas, NV
15 November 2026

143ee22a-4813-43f7-8755-ae949e8b7833R04